Enfield Librarie		
Branch: ETL		
07/14		

ISBN: 9781290541442

Published by:
HardPress Publishing
8345 NW 66TH ST #2561
MIAMI FL 33166-2626

Email: info@hardpress.net
Web: http://www.hardpress.net

THE LIBRARY
OF
THE UNIVERSITY
OF CALIFORNIA
LOS ANGELES

THE CITY OF FEAR

London Borough of Enfield	
91200000462980	
Askews & Holts	Jul-2014
	£12.95

THE CITY OF FEAR
AND OTHER POEMS
By GILBERT FRANKAU

LONDON
CHATTO & WINDUS
MCMXVIII

CONTENTS

	PAGE
THE CITY OF FEAR	3
HOW RIFLEMAN BROWN CAME TO VALHALLA	15
THE INN OF A THOUSAND DREAMS	23

THE GUNS—

(1) The Voice of the Slaves	31
(2) Headquarters	33
(3) Gun-Teams	35
(4) Eyes in the Air	37
(5) Signals	40
(6) The Observers	42
(7) Ammunition Column	44
(8) The Voice of the Guns	46

The City of Fear.

YPRES
January, 1916

THE CITY OF FEAR

THIS was a city once: women lived here;
   Their voices were low to their lovers, o'nights by the murmuring waters;
Their hands were busied with home—mothers and daughters,
Sisters and wives:
Now, the shell dives
To scatter anew the shattered remains of the homes that their hands made
   dear;
Fear
Walks nakéd at noonday's clear
Where the shopman proffered his wares to the loitering street,
Where the Mass was read.
Above,
The war-birds beat
And whistle: and love
And laughter and work and the hum of the city are utterly dead.

Never a barge
Ruffles the long canals : the lock-gates rot,
Letting thin runnels spout :
Never the plash of a rope in the reeds nor the pash of a hoof on the marge
Crack of whip, nor the shout
Of driver gladdens the quiet : the foul weeds knot,
Strangling the sluggish flow of the waterway ;
Slime of decay
Clots on the banks where the shell-holes cut deep and the shored edges crumble,
Clots on the piers of the bridges that echo to transport wheels' rumble
At fall of the night
When no light
Is a-gleam—
Till the sudden flame from a gun-muzzle crimsons the ebon glass of the stream.

Here, where the rails
Ran straight and glittering, linking city to teeming prosperous plain,
Mist and the rain
And long disuse have rusted the glint of the steel that the wheels made shining ;
Flame and steel have twisted the steel from the lines of its fair designing :
Gold with grain,
Shone the fields once when the harvest of peacetime was ripe to the sun for the flails ;

Green and red,
Gleamed the lights once when the track was a-quiver, a-roar with the
    freight and the mails—
But the life of the farm and the life of the field and the traffic of peacetime
    are utterly dead.

The brown roads run
Bare to the sun;
Not a cart
Jingles in through the gates that our torn graves guard
To the mart;
Never a peasant girl passes and smiles with raised eyes for a greeting,
Never men clink at the cottage the cup of the wayfarers' meeting;
(Strown
Into heaps by the roadside the cottages, blown
And riven by shell-fire, and scarred!)
Only at night, when the dank mists arise and the gaze of our watchers is
    hidden,
Comes tramp and muttered cursing of infantry, rush of horse ridden
In fear of the dark—
For who knows how the far shell may swerve or the blind bullet hiss to its
    mark!

Roadway, water or rail, the life has died in the veins,
As life is dead at the breast;
Only remains
The hollow corpse of a city, slashed and gutted of war,

A grinning skeleton-city, mocking the eye from afar
With a hangman's jest—
With tower and chimney and gable where scarcely swallows might rest.
Look well,
Ye that shall die as we died!
Is there roof of these roofs to guard your heads from the wind or the rain
    or the sun?
Is there wall unholed of the gun,
Or street unpitted of shell?
Is there place where Man might abide . . .
Has the house he built for his scornful gods been proof 'gainst the shafts
    of Hell?

Ruin is over it all, hideous, complete:
Street upon street;
House upon house that was gay with the patter of lost children's feet,
Whose windows were mirrors of lamp-light to beckon its worker returning
To welcome of arms and of eyes, to the warmth of the home-fire's bright
    burning;
Palace and cot;
Their charred beams rot
And their rent walls gape as they totter, betraying the havoc within—
Iron and tin,
Brickwork and stone,
Glasswork and tilework and woodwork to refuse-heaps battered and spilt
    and o'erthrown.

Through the storied square—
Where aforetime the belfry spired
In a moonbeam-fretted splendour of stone that was pride of a guild long dead,
Where the glory of glass
Was fired
By the orange flames of a thousand candles ablaze on altar and shrine,
Till the quiet beauty of perfect things was warm to the soul as wine—
Men pass
Hurriedly, fearfully, quickening the footstep, barely averting the head
To vision in dread
A gleaming, terrible desert, pit-falled with shadow-wells,
Blasted and bored by the shells,
Jaggéd with rocks :—
For the steel has stripped
And ravished the splendours of graven stone, the ruby glory of glass,
Till apse and gargoyle, buttress and nave,
Reredos, pillar, and crypt,
Lie tumbled and crumbled to monstrous ruins of splintering granite-blocks . . .
Over the grave
Of the work that was spared for the sake of the work by the Vandals of
 elder wars,
Only one tattered pinnacle leers to the calm of the outraged stars.

This is the City of Fear!
Death
Has ringed her walls with his sickle, has choked her streets with his breath ;

In her cellars the rat feeds red
On the bodies of those whom their own roofbeams betrayed to him as they
    fled—
For none live here
Save you that shall die, as we died, for the city, and we, your dead
Whom God for the sake of our one brave dream has garnered into His
    hand . . .
Will He give them to understand,
The proud and the thankless cities we left in a sheltered land?

Should we care at all?
Should we not turn and take rest from our labours;
Here, where you buried us, sleep?
Forget the dream that was cheap at life, forget the wounds and the pain;
Never again
Remember the call
That came to our souls in the sheltered cities, drawing us over the deep?
Remember in vain!

Gladly we came—
From peaceful homeland village; from the raw dun dusty town,
Where sun of the North drops down
In purple behind the prairie; from the pulsing plate-glass streets,
That are bright with the girls of our younger nations at southern rim of the
    sea;

From lazy tropic townships, where light of day is a flame,
And the night wave beats
In fire on the scented foreshores, and the cicad sings in the tree;
From the gay gray mother of all our cities, at ease on her banks of Thame—
Came and died,
Here
In the City of Fear.

Gladly we died,
But in death is no peace for us,
Rest nor release for us.

Had you buried us deep--
You whom we left to fulfill us the task that was stricken out of our power—
Had you rolled the battle-tide back from our city, till only the growl of your guns
Fell faint on our ears as the baying of hounds that were hunting over the hill,
Perchance we might sleep:
But day upon day that grows weary, and hour upon slow-footed hour,
The long year runs;
And ever the foeman beats at the gates and batters at rampart and tower
And our souls are unquiet, for the voice of our dreaming will neither rest nor be still.

Our spirits fret
Through the troubled night,
To each sputter of rifle-fire,
To each clink of your transport wheels;
Fret
To the roar and flash of your sleepless guns, to the tread of your feet in the
    mire,
To each soaring light
That reveals,
In a silvern silhouette,
House and tree and the hump of a crest and the broken tooth of a spire;
Fret,
By day when the high planes drone,
And the great shells throb through the void,
And the trenches blur in the gray;
Fret, and pray
That the hour be near
When the bonds of the foeman that hold us be utterly broke and destroyed,
And ours alone,
The City of Fear.

How can we rest,
Knowing it all unaccomplished, the vow that was dear to us dying?
How can we sleep or be still
In our tombs that are spattered and ploughed by the shell-bursts and shaken
    by salvoes replying,

Till dead bones thrill;
Till our souls break forth from the grave—
Unshriven, unblest—
To flutter and shrill
Down the winds that murmur and moan in the ruins our bodies were tortured
    to save.

Ye that remain,
Have ye no pity
For us that are sped?
Was it then vain,
Vain that we bartered our youth for the walls of the desolate city,
Bartered the red
Life's blood, and the hopes that were dearer than blood and the uttermost
    faith that was given us?
Death hath not shriven us . . .
Shrive ye your dead!

How Rifleman Brown Came to Valhalla.

NEUVE ÉGLISE
June, 1916

HOW RIFLEMAN BROWN CAME TO VALHALLA

TO the lower Hall of Valhalla, to the heroes of no renown,
    Relieved from his spell at the listening-post, came Rifleman Joseph Brown.
With never a rent in his khaki nor smear of blood on his face,
He flung his pack from his shoulders, and made for an empty place.

The Killer-men of Valhalla looked up from the banquet-board
At the unfouled breech of his rifle, at the unfleshed point of his sword;
And the unsung dead of the trenches, the kings who have never a crown,
Demanded his pass to Valhalla from Rifleman Joseph Brown.

"*Who comes, unhit, to the party?*" A one-legged Corporal spoke,
And the gashed heads nodded approval through the rings of the Endless Smoke:
"*Who comes for the beer and the Woodbines of the never-closed Canteen,*
"*With the barrack-shine on his bayonet and a full-charged magazine?*"

Then Rifleman Brown looked round him at the nameless men of the Line—
At the wounds of the shell and the bullet, at the burns of the bomb and the mine;
At the tunics, virgin of medals but crimson-clotted with blood;
At the ankle-boots and the puttees, caked stiff with the Flanders mud;
At the myriad short Lee-Enfields that crowded the rifle-rack,
Each with its blade to the sword-boss brown, and its muzzle powder-black:

And Rifleman Brown said never a word; yet he felt in the soul of his soul
His right to the beer of the lower Hall, though he came to drink of it, whole;
His right to the fags of the free Canteen, to a seat at the banquet-board,
Though he came to the men who had killed their man, with never a man to his sword.

"*Who speaks for the stranger Rifleman, O boys of the free Canteen?*
Who passes the chap with the unmaimed limbs and the kit that is far too clean?"
The gashed heads eyed him above their beers, the gashed lips sucked at their smoke:
There were three at the board of his own platoon, but not a man of them spoke.

His mouth was mad for the tankard froth and the biting whiff of a fag,
But he knew that he might not speak for himself to the dead men who do not brag.

A gun-butt crashed on the gateway, a man came staggering in ;
His head was cleft with a great red wound from the temple-bone to the chin,
His blade was dyed to the bayonet-boss with the clots that were scarcely dry ;
And he cried to the men who had killed their man :

         " Who passes the Rifleman ? I !
By the four I slew, by the shell I stopped, if my feet be not too late,
I speak the word for Rifleman Brown that a chap may speak for his mate."

The dead of lower Valhalla, the heroes of dumb renown,
They pricked their ears to a tale of the earth as they set their tankards down.

" My mate was on sentry this evening when the General happened along
And asked what he'd do in a gas-attack. Joe told him : 'Beat on the gong.'
'What else ? '
   'Open fire, Sir,' Joe answered.
         'Good God, man,' our General said,
' By the time you'd beaten that bloodstained gong the chances are you'd be
   dead.
Just think, lad.' 'Gas helmet, of course, Sir.' ' Yes, damn it, and *gas helmet
   first.*'
So Joe stood dumb to attention, and wondered why he'd been cursed."

The gashed heads turned to the Rifleman, and now it seemed that they knew
Why the face that had never a smear of blood was stained to the jawbones,
   blue.

"He was posted again at midnight." The scarred heads craned to the voice,
As the man with the blood-red bayonet spoke up for the mate of his choice.
"You know what it's like in a listening-post, the Very candles aflare,
Their bullets smacking the sand-bags, our Vickers combing your hair,
How your ears and your eyes get jumpy, till each known tuft that you scan
Moves and crawls in the shadows till you'd almost swear it was man;
You know how you peer and snuff at the night when the North-East gas-winds blow."
"*By the One who made us and maimed us*" quoth lower Valhalla "*we know!*"

"Sudden, out of the blackness, sudden as Hell, there came
Roar and rattle of rifles, spurts of machine-gun flame;
And Joe stood up in the forward sap to try and fathom the game.
Sudden, their shells come screaming; sudden, his nostrils sniff
The sickening reek of the rotten pears, the death that kills with a whiff.
Death! and he knows it certain, as he bangs on his cartridge-case,
With the gas-cloud's claws at his windpipe and the gas cloud's wings on his face. . . .
We heard his gong in our dug-out, he only whacked on it twice,
We whipped our gas-bags over our heads, and manned the step in a trice—
For the cloud would have caught us as sure as Fate if he'd taken the Staff's advice."

His head was cleft with a great red wound from the chin to the temple-bone,
But his voice was as clear as a sounding gong, "I'll be damned if I'll drink alone,

'Not even in lower Valhalla ! Is he free of your free Canteen,
My mate who comes with the unfleshed point and the full-charged magazine?"

The gashed heads rose at the Rifleman o'er the rings of the Endless Smoke,
And loud as the roar of a thousand guns Valhalla's answer broke,
And loud as the crash of a thousand shells their tankards clashed on the board:
"*He is free of the mess of the Killer-men, your mate of the unfleshed sword;*
For we know the worth of his deed on earth; as we know the speed of the death
Which catches its man by the back of the throat and gives him water for breath;
As we know how the hand at the helmet-cloth may tarry seconds too long,
When the very life of the front-line trench is staked on the beat of a gong.
By the four you slew, by the case he smote, by the gray gas-cloud and the green,
We pass your mate for the Endless Smoke and the beer of the free Canteen."

In the lower hall of Valhalla, with the heroes of no renown,
With our nameless dead of the Marne and the Aisne, of Mons, and of Wipers town,
With the men who killed ere they died for us, sits Rifleman Joseph Brown.

The Inn of a Thousand Dreams.

NEUVE ÉGLISE
June, 1916

THE INN OF A THOUSAND DREAMS

Where the road climbs free from the marsh and the sea
  To the last rose sunset-gleams,
Twixt a fold and a fold of the Kentish wold
  Stands the Inn of a Thousand Dreams.

NO man may ride with map for guide
  And win that tavern-door;
As none shall come by rule of thumb
  To our blue-bells' dancing-floor :
For no path leads through Churchyard Meads
  And the fringes of Daffodil Wood,
To the heart of the glade where the flower-folk played
  In the days when the gods were good.

Who hastes our wold with naught but gold,
  Who seeks but food and wine,
The wood-folk wise shall blind his eyes
  To the creaking tavern-sign ;

He shall know the goad of the folk of the road
    And his led wheels shall not find
The gabled beams that sheltered our dreams
    In the nights when the gods were kind.

We had never a chart save our own sure heart
    And the summoning sunset-gleams,
When you rode with me from the marsh and the sea
    To the Inn of a Thousand Dreams.

No sign-post showed the curved hill-road
    Our purring engines clomb,
From where dead forts of dying ports
    Loomed gray against gray foam:
We had never a book for the way we took,
    But the oast-house chimney-vanes
Stretched beckoning hands o'er the lambing-lands
    To point us their Kentish lanes.

As certain-true our track we flew,
    As nesting swiftsures flit;
By stream and down and county-town,
    And orchards blossom-lit:
For Pan's own heels were guiding our wheels,
    And Pan's self checked our speed
In the spire-crowned street where the by-ways meet,
    For a sign of the place decreed.

Rose-impearled o'er a wonder-world
    Glowed the last of the sunset-gleams;
And we knew that fate had led to the gate
    Of the Inn of our Thousand Dreams.

Who needs must pique with kitchen-freak
    His jaded appetite,
He shall not know our set cloth's snow,
    Our primrose candle-light:
We had never a need of the waiter-breed
    Or an alien bandsman's blare,
When we pledged a toast to our landlord host
    As he served us his goodwife's fare.

In right of guest, they gave their best:
    No hireling hands outspread
White bridal-dress from linen-press,
    To drape our marriage bed:
They had never a thought for the price we brought,
    The simple folk and the fine,
Who made us free of their hostelry
    In the nights when all dreams were mine.

When the trench-lights rise to the storm-dark skies
    Where the gun-flash flickers and gleams,
My soul flies free o'er an English sea
    To the Inn of a Thousand Dreams.

Once more we flit, hands passion-knit,
    By marsh and murmuring shore,
By Tenterden and Bennenden,
    To our own tavern-door;
And again we go, where the sunsets glow
    On the beech-tree's silvern plinth,
Down woodpaths set with violet
    And Spring's wild hyacinth.

Once more we pass, by roads of grass,
    To find for our delight
Trim garden-plots, and shepherd's cots—
    Half-timbered, black-and-white . . .
There is never one gash of a shrapnel-splash
    On the walls of the street we roam,
Where the forge-irons ring for our welcoming
    As the twilight calls us home.

Till the trench-lights pale on the gray dawn-veil
    Of the first wan sunrise-gleams,
My soul would bide with its spirit-bride
    At the Inn of a Thousand Dreams.

Once more I press, in tenderness,
    (Dear God, that dreams were true!)
Your finger-tips against these lips
    Your own red-rose lips knew,

In the middle night when your throat gleamed white
    On your dark hairs' pillowed sheen,
And your eyes were the pools that a moonbeam cools
    For the feet of a fäery queen.

Woman o'mine, heart's anodyne
    Against unkindly fate,
Love's aureole about my soul,
    Wife, mistress, comrade, mate!
I stretch ghost-hands from the stricken lands
    Where my earth-bound body lies,
To touch your fair smooth brow, your hair,
    Your lips, your sleeping eyes:

You are living-warm in the crook of my arm,
    You are pearl in the firelight-gleams . . .
Till the blind night rocks with the cannon-shocks
    That shatter a thousand dreams.

The Guns.

LOOS
September, 1915

THE VOICE OF THE SLAVES

We are the slaves of the guns,
  Serfs to the dominant things;
Ours are the eyes and the ears,
  And the brains of their messagings.

OURS are the hands that unleash
    The blind gods that raven by night,
The lords of the terror at dawn,
  When the landmarks are blotted from sight
By the lit curdled churnings of smoke;
  When the lost trenches crumble and spout
Into loud roaring fountains of flame;
  Till, their prison walls down, with a shout
And a cheer, ordered line after line,
  Black specks on the barrage of gray
That we lift—as they leap—to the clock,
  Our infantry storm to the fray.

These are our masters, the slim
  Grim muzzles that irk in the pit;
That chafe for the rushing of wheels,
  For the teams plunging madly to bit
As the gunners swing down to unkey,
  For the trails sweeping half-circle-right,

For the six breech-blocks clashing as one
    To a target viewed clear on the sight—
Dun masses, the shells search and tear
    Into fragments that bunch as they run—
For the hour of the red battle-harvest,
    The dream of the slaves of the gun.

We have bartered our souls to the guns;
    Every fibre of body and brain
Have we trained to them, chained to them. Serfs?
    Aye! but proud of the weight of our chain—
Of our backs that are bowed to their workings,
    To hide them and guard and disguise—
Of our ears that are deafened with service,
    Of hands that are scarred, and of eyes
Grown hawklike with marking their prey—
    Of wings that are ripped as with swords
When we hover, the turn of a blade
    From the death that is sweet to our lords.

By the ears and the eyes and the brain,
    By the limbs and the hands and the wings,
We are slaves to our masters the guns . . .
    But their slaves are the masters of kings!

HEADQUARTERS

A LEAGUE and a league from the trenches—from the traversed maze
    of the lines,
Where daylong the sniper watches and daylong the bullet whines,
And the cratered earth is in travail with mines and with countermines—

Here, where haply some woman dreamed, (are those her roses that bloom
In the garden beyond the windows of my littered working-room?)
We have decked the map for our masters as a bride is decked for the groom.

Fair, on each lettered numbered square—cross-road and mound and wire,
Loophole, redoubt and emplacement—lie the targets their mouths desire;
Gay with purples and browns and blues, have we traced them their arcs of fire.

And ever the type-keys clatter; and ever our keen wires bring
Word from the watchers a-crouch below, word from the watchers a-wing:
And ever we hear the distant growl of our hid guns thundering.

Hear it hardly, and turn again to our maps, where the trench-lines crawl,
Red on the gray and each with a sign for the ranging shrapnel's fall—
Snakes that our masters shall scotch at dawn, as is written here on the wall.

For the weeks of our waiting draw to a close. . . . There is scarcely a leaf
    astir
In the garden beyond my windows, where the twilight shadows blurr
The blaze of some woman's roses. . . .
                      "Bombardment orders, sir."

GUN-TEAMS

THEIR rugs are sodden, their heads are down, their tails are turned to the storm:
(Would you know them, you that groomed them in the sleek fat days of peace,
When the tiles rang to their pawings in the lighted stalls, and warm,
Now the foul clay cakes on breeching strap and clogs the quick-release?)

The blown rain stings, there is never a star, the tracks are rivers of slime:
(You must harness-up by guesswork with a failing torch for light,
Instep-deep in unmade standings; for it's active-service time,
And our resting weeks are over, and we move the guns to-night.)

The iron tyres slither, the traces sag, their blind hooves stumble and slide
They are war-worn, they are weary, soaked with sweat and sopped with rain:
(You must hold them, you must help them, swing your lead and centre wide
Where the greasy granite *pavé* peters out to squelching drain.)

There is shrapnel bursting a mile in front on the road that the guns must
   take :
(You are thoughtful, you are nervous, you are shifting in your seat,
As you watch the ragged feathers flicker orange, flame and break) :
But the teams are pulling steady down the battered village street.

You have shod them cold, and their coats are long, and their bellies stiff
   with the mud ;
They have done with gloss and polish, but the fighting heart's unbroke . . .
We, who saw them hobbling after us down white roads flecked with blood,
Patient, wondering why we left them, till we lost them in the smoke ;

Who have felt them shiver between our knees, when the shells rain black
   from the skies,
When the bursting terrors find us and the lines stampede as one ;
Who have watched the pierced limbs quiver and the pain in stricken eyes ;
Know the worth of humble servants, foolish-faithful to their gun.

EYES IN THE AIR

OUR guns are a league behind us, our target a mile below,
And there's never a cloud to blind us from the haunts of our lurking foe—
Sunk pit whence his shrapnel tore us, support-trench crest-concealed,
As clear as the charts before us, his ramparts lie revealed.
His panicked watchers spy us, a droning threat in the void;
Their whistling shells outfly us—puff upon puff, deployed
Across the green beneath us, across the flanking gray,
In fume and fire to sheath us and baulk us of our prey.
   Below, beyond, above her,
    Their iron web is spun:
   Flicked but unsnared we hover,
    Edged planes against the sun:
   Eyes in the air above his lair,
    The hawks that guide the gun!

No word from earth may reach us, save, white against the ground,
The strips outspread to teach us whose ears are deaf to sound :
But down the winds that sear us, athwart our engine's shriek,
We send—and know they hear us, the ranging guns we speak.
Our visored eyeballs show us their answering pennant, broke
Eight thousand feet below us, a whorl of flame-stabbed smoke—
The burst that hangs to guide us, while numbed gloved fingers tap
From wireless key beside us the circles of the map.
  Line—target—short or over—
   Come, plain as clock hands run,
  Words from the birds that hover,
   Unblinded, tail to sun ;
  Words out of air to range them fair,
   From hawks that guide the gun !

Your flying shells have failed you, your landward guns are dumb:
Since earth hath naught availed you, these skies be open! Come,
Where, wild to meet and mate you, flame in their beaks for breath,
Black doves! the white hawks wait you on the wind-tossed boughs of death.
These boughs be cold without you, our hearts are hot for this,
Our wings shall beat about you, our scorching breath shall kiss;
Till, fraught with that we gave you, fulfilled of our desire,
You bank—too late to save you from biting beaks of fire—
    Turn sideways from your lover,
     Shudder and swerve and run,
    Tilt; stagger; and plunge over
     Ablaze against the sun:
    Doves dead in air, who clomb to dare
     The hawks that guide the gun!

SIGNALS

THE hot wax drips from the flares
On the scrawled pink forms that litter
The bench where he sits; the glitter
Of stars is framed by the sandbags atop of the dug-out stairs.
And the lagging watch hands creep;
And his cloaked mates murmur in sleep—
Forms he can wake with a kick—
And he hears, as he plays with the pressel-switch, the strapped receiver click
On his ear that listens, listens;
And the candle-flicker glistens
On the rounded brass of the switch-board where the red wires cluster thick.

   Wires from the earth, from the air;
   Wires that whisper and chatter,
   At night, when the trench-rats patter
And nibble among the rations and scuttle back to their lair;
   Wires that are never at rest;
   For the linesmen tap them and test,
   And ever they tremble with tone;
And he knows from a hundred signals the buzzing call of his own,
   The breaks and the vibrant stresses,—
   The F, and the G, and the Esses,
That call his hand to the answering key and his mouth to the microphone.

   For always the laid guns fret
   On the words that his mouth shall utter,
   When rifle and Maxim stutter
And the rockets volley to starward from the spurting parapet;
   And always his ear must hark
   To the voices out of the dark;
   For the whisper over the wire,
From the bombed and the battered trenches where the wounded redden the mire;
   For a sign to waken the thunder
   Which shatters the night in sunder
With the flash of the leaping muzzles and the beat of battery-fire.

THE OBSERVERS

ERE the last light that leaps the night has hung and shone and died,
  While yet the breast-high fog of dawn is swathed about the plain,
By hedge and track our slaves go back, the waning stars for guide—
  Eyes of our mouths, the mists have cleared, the guns would speak again!

Faint on the ear that strains to hear, their orders trickle down:
  "Degrees—twelve—left of zero line—corrector one three eight—
Three thousand." . . . Shift our trails, and lift the muzzles that shall drown
  The rifle's idle chatter when our sendings detonate.

Sending or still, these serve our will; the hidden eyes that mark,
  From gutted farm, from laddered tree that scans the furrowed slope,
From coigns of slag whose pit-props sag on burrowed ways and dark,
  In open trench where sandbags mask the steady periscope.

Waking, they know the instant foe, the bullets phutting by,
 The blurring lens, the sodden map, the wires that leak or break:
Sleeping, they dream of shells that scream adown a sunless sky . . .
 And the splinters patter round them in their dug-outs as they wake.

Not theirs, the wet glad bayonet, the red and racing hour,
 The rush that clears the bombing-post with knife and hand-grenade;
Not theirs the zest when, steel to breast, the last survivors cower:
 Yet can ye hold the ground ye won, save these be there to aid;

These, that observe the shell's far swerve, these of the quiet voice
 That bids "go on," repeats the range, corrects for fuze or line? . . .
Though dour the task their masters ask, what room for thought or choice
 This is ours by right of service, heedless gift of youthful eyne.

Careless they give while yet they live: the dead we tasked too sore
 Bear witness we were naught begrudged of riches, naught of youth;
Careless they gave; across their grave our calling salvoes roar,
 And those we maimed come back to us in proof our dead speak truth.

AMMUNITION COLUMN

I AM only a cog in a giant machine, a link of an endless chain:—
    And the rounds are drawn, and the rounds are fired, and the empties return again;
Railroad, lorry, and limber, battery, column, and park;
To the shelf where the set fuze waits the breech, from the quay where the shells embark.
We have watered and fed, and eaten our beef: the long dull day drags by,
As I sit here watching our "Archibalds" *strafing* an empty sky;
Puff and flash on the far-off blue round the speck one guesses the plane—
Smoke and spark of the gun-machine that is fed by the endless chain.

I am only a cog in a giant machine, a little link of the chain,
Waiting a word from the wagon-lines that the guns are hungry again:—
Column-wagon to battery-wagon, and battery-wagon to gun;
To the loader kneeling 'twixt trail and wheel from the shops where the steam-lathes run.
There's a lone mule braying against the line where the mud cakes fetlock-deep;
There's a lone soul humming a hint of a song in the barn where the drivers sleep;
And I hear the pash of the orderly's horse as he canters him down the lane—
Another cog in the gun-machine, a link in the self-same chain.

I am only a cog in a giant machine, but a vital link of the chain;
And the Captain has sent from the wagon-line to fill his wagons again:—
From wagon-limber to gunpit dump; from loader's forearm at breech,
To the working party that melts away when the shrapnel bullets screech.
So the restless section pulls out once more, in column of route from the right,
At the tail of a blood-red afternoon; so the flux of another night
Bears back the wagons we fill at dawn to the sleeping column again—
Cog on cog in the gun-machine, link on link in the chain!

THE VOICE OF THE GUNS

WE are the guns, and your masters! Saw ye our flashes?
Heard ye the scream of our shells in the night, and the shuddering
 crashes?
Saw ye our work by the roadside, the shrouded things lying,
Moaning to God that He made them—the maimed and the dying?
Husbands or sons,
Fathers or lovers, we break them. We are the guns!

We are the guns and ye serve us. Dare ye grow weary,
Steadfast at night-time, at noon-time; or waking, when dawn winds blow
 dreary
Over the fields and the flats and the reeds of the barrier-water,
To wait on the hour of our choosing, the minute decided for slaughter?
Swift, the clock runs;
Yea, to the ultimate second. *Stand to your guns!*

. We are the guns, and we need you; here, in the timbered
Pits that are screened by the crest, and the copse where at dusk ye
unlimbered;
Pits that one found us—and, finding, gave life (Did he flinch from the
giving?);
Laboured by moonlight when wraith of the dead brooded yet o'er the living;
Ere, with the sun's
Rising, the sorrowful spirit abandoned its guns.

Who but the guns shall avenge him? *Battery—Action!*
Load us and lay to the centremost hair of the dial-sight's refraction;
Set your quick hands to our levers to compass the sped soul's assoiling;
Brace your taut limbs to the shock when the thrust of the barrel recoiling
Deafens and stuns!
Vengeance is ours for our servants: trust ye the guns!

Least of our bond-slaves or greatest, grudge ye the burden?
Hard, is this service of ours which has only our service for guerdon:
Grow the limbs lax, and unsteady the hands, which aforetime we trusted?
Flawed, the clear crystal of sight; and the clean steel of hardihood rusted?
Dominant ones,
Are we not tried serfs and proven—true to our guns?

Ye are the guns! Are we worthy? Shall not these speak for us,
Out of the woods where the tree-trunks are slashed with the vain bolts that seek for us,
Thunder of batteries firing in unison, swish of shell flighting,
Hissing that rushes to silence and breaks to the thud of alighting;
    Death that outruns
Horseman and foot? Are we justified? Answer, O guns!

Yea! by your works are ye justified—toil unrelievéd;
Manifold labours, co-ordinate each to the sending achievéd;
Discipline, not of the feet but the soul, unremitting, unfeignéd;
Tortures unholy by flame and by maiming, known, faced, and disdainéd;
    Courage that shuns
Only foolhardiness; even by these, are ye worthy your guns.

Wherefore,—and unto ye only—power hath been given;
Yea! beyond man, over men, over desolate cities and riven;
Yea! beyond space, over earth and the seas and the sky's high dominions;
Yea! beyond time, over Hell and the fiends and the Death-angel's pinions.
    Vigilant ones,
Loose them, and shatter, and spare not. We are the guns!

E

SOME PRESS OPINIONS
OF OTHER BOOKS BY
GILBERT FRANKAU

SOME PRESS OPINIONS OF
BOOKS BY GILBERT FRANKAU

ONE OF US
A NOVEL IN VERSE

Seventh Edition. Cr. 8vo, boards, 3s. 6d. net.

"A modern Don Juan—the adventures of a reckless young man in his way through the world. In this form of verse, light, satiric, worldly and picturesque, Mr. Gilbert Frankau is a master."—W. L. COURTNEY in *The Daily Telegraph*.

"One of the finest satirical poems in the language."—*Evening Standard*.

"A triumph of audacity."—SIDNEY DARK in *The Daily Express*.

"It is a great satire—a thing unique."—JAMES DOUGLAS in *The Star*.

"As witty, as cynical, as unblushingly impudent as Don Juan's self."—*Academy*.

"TID'APA"
(WHAT *DOES* IT MATTER)

Fourth Impression, Demy 8vo, boards, 3s. 6d. net.

"Dramatic and full of vivid pictures."—*New Statesman*.

"A strange and powerful piece of work. The satire bites keenly."—*Sunday Times*.

"The tale is told with a vivid sense of reality, and in its tenser passages is both dramatic and poetic."—*Glasgow Herald*.

"The poem is extraordinarily dramatic, very powerful, written with admirable restraint."—*Tatler*.

"The powerful and poignant tale. . . . A Kiplingesque tragi-satire which made a sensation."—*Illustrated London News*.

LONDON: CHATTO & WINDUS

SOME PRESS OPINIONS OF
BOOKS BY GILBERT FRANKAU

THE CITY OF FEAR

Fourth Impression. Pott 4to, cloth, 3s. 6d. net.

" In times of peace Mr. Frankau would compose a satirical novel in verse, tell bitingly of the silly things in a stupid life, laugh at folly, and arrest us with an evident power. Now he is with the guns, an adjutant with the Royal Field Artillery in Flanders. Here, then, is something powerful, very real from the war, by no means to be overlooked by anyone who reads. Nothing of its kind may be done better until the guns are quiet again."—*Daily Telegraph.*

" These verses are singularly vigorous and telling. Mr. Frankau has personified the guns, and has made their efforts and achievements live in every detail."—*Athenæum.*

" These poems, written in the fighting line, have the Kipling joy of action, the Kipling appreciation of the importance of the smallest cog in the wheel. Let me quote as an example the first verse of 'The Voice of the Guns' . . . That really is very splendid, as indeed is the whole of this little book."—*Daily Express.*

" A poem that no reader, we believe, will finish without a lump in the throat—' How Rifleman Brown came to Valhalla.' This is surely the finest thing Mr. Frankau has written."—*To-Day.*

" As yet it is a gunner—Captain Gilbert Frankau—who has written the best ballad of war flying. *Eyes in the Air* is a brilliant picture of aeroplanes at the work of registering."—*Land and Water.*

LONDON : CHATTO & WINDUS

SOME PRESS OPINIONS OF
BOOKS BY GILBERT FRANKAU

THE WOMAN OF THE HORIZON

Third Impression. Cr. 8vo, cloth, 6s. net.

"Mr. Gilbert Frankau's first novel in prose, is certainly a very exciting and highly-coloured production. It leaves on one a whirling impression that defies definition. The general effect is fascinating."—*Morning Post.*

"It is well written, and, long though it is, is never dull."—*The Scotsman.*

"The picture of the Taj Mahal is a little masterpiece of suggestion, and there is a storm at sea, described from the point of view of the passengers, which is scarcely to be matched outside the pages of Mr. Joseph Conrad. The moral of the story is a sound one."—*Daily Telegraph.*

"It is an unusual book well worth pondering."—*Glasgow Herald.*

"Mr. Gilbert Frankau achieved an uncommon story, a mirror that deeply reflects life in many aspects."—*Ladies' Field.*

"I am sure I never put the book down until I had finished it, and that I followed the loving hero upon his voyages with unswerving interest and excitement. I take off my hat to Gilbert Frankau, who is well come to the rank of novelist, and deserves the V.C. which stands for very clever."—*Truth.*

"Vivid realisation of local colour not less varied than well observed."—*The Observer.*

"The reader will be entranced by the author's language. He writes like a poet."—*Liverpool Post.*

LONDON: CHATTO & WINDUS

PRINTED BY
THE DE LA MORE PRESS LTD.
32 GEORGE STREET, HANOVER SQUARE
LONDON W. 1

UNIVERSITY OF CALIFORNIA LIBRARY
Los Angeles

This book is DUE on the last date stamped below.

Form L9–40m-7,'56(C790s4)444

THE LIBRARY
UNIVERSITY OF CALIFORNIA
LOS ANGELES

PR   Frankau -
6011   City of fear
F85c

PR
6011
F85c

ImTheStory.com

Personalized Classic Books in many genre's

Unique gift for kids, partners, friends, colleagues

Customize:

- Character Names
- Upload your own front/back cover images (optional)
- Inscribe a personal message/dedication on the inside page (optional)

Customize many titles Including
- Alice in Wonderland
- Romeo and Juliet
- The Wizard of Oz
- A Christmas Carol
- Dracula
- Dr. Jekyll & Mr. Hyde
- And more...

Lightning Source UK Ltd.
Milton Keynes UK
UKOW04f1057220614

233847UK00013B/123/P